PREHISTORIC
FACTS & LISTS

2

PREHISTORIC FACTS & LISTS

Sarah Khan

Edited by Phillip Clarke

Designed by
Luke Sargent and Karen Tomlins

Digital imagery by Keith Furnival

Consultants: Dr David Martill,
University of Portsmouth
and Darren Naish

Managing designer: Ruth Russell
Series editor: Judy Tatchell

Internet Links

Throughout this book, we have suggested interesting Web sites where you can find out more about the prehistoric world. To visit the sites, go to the **Usborne Quicklinks Web site** at **www.usborne-quicklinks.com** and type the keywords "prehistoric facts". There you will find links to click on to take you to all the sites. Here are some of the things you can do on the Web sites:

• Swim with prehistoric sharks.

• Play a game to find out how you would survive as a dinosaur.

• Uncover the mysteries of an ancient Turkish village.

Site availability

The links in **Usborne Quicklinks** are regularly reviewed and updated, but occasionally you may get a message that a site is unavailable. This might be temporary, so try again later, or even the next day. If any of the sites close down, we will, if possible, replace them with suitable alternatives, so you will always find an up-to-date list of sites in **Usborne Quicklinks**.

Internet safety

When using the Internet, please make sure you follow these guidelines:

• Ask your parent's or guardian's permission before you connect to the Internet.

• If you write a message in a Web site guest book or on a Web site message board, do not include any personal information such as your full name, address or telephone number, and ask an adult before you give your e-mail address.

• If a Web site asks you to log in or register by typing your name or e-mail address, ask permission from an adult first.

• If you do receive an e-mail from someone you don't know, tell an adult and do not reply to the e-mail.

• Never arrange to meet anyone you have talked to on the Internet.

Note for parents and guardians

The Web sites described in this book are regularly reviewed and the links in **Usborne Quicklinks** are updated. However, the content of a Web site may change at any time and Usborne Publishing is not responsible for the content on any Web site other than its own.

We recommend that children are supervised while on the Internet, that they do not use Internet Chat Rooms, and that you use Internet filtering software to block unsuitable material. Please ensure that your children read and follow the safety guidelines printed on the left. For more information, see the **Net Help** area on the **Usborne Quicklinks** Web site.

Computer not essential

If you don't have access to the Internet, don't worry. This book is a complete, superb, self-contained reference book on its own.

Contents

What is Prehistory?

History is the story of human beings that is learned from written records. It goes back about 5,500 years to the first known writing.

Prehistory is even older than that. It is the story of life on Earth that is learned from the remains of animals and plants. Prehistory begins around 3,000 million years ago with the first known living things.

The Sun's heat and light made life on Earth possible.

Fit for life

It took millions of years for conditions on Earth to become suitable for life to begin. To survive, living things need the right amounts of light and heat from the Sun, along with food, water and oxygen.

4,600 million years ago

A cloud of dust and gases swirling round the Sun started to shrink and heat up. It then changed into a ball of liquid rock.

4,000 million years ago

The ball of rock slowly cooled down to form the Earth. Thick clouds gathered over the surface and rain began to fall.

3,500 million years ago

It rained for thousands of years. The rainwater made rivers and oceans.

3,000 million years ago

The first living things grew in the sea. They were made of just one cell each and were similar to bacteria or germs.

INTERNET LINK

For a link to a Web site where you can take an interactive tour through the story of the universe go to **www.usborne-quicklinks.com**

The Earth was formed 4,600 million years ago. If you counted to 4,600 million and each number took you one second to recite, you would be counting for over 146 years.

Measuring time

The Earth's story goes back so far that scientists measure it in periods of millions of years. Dates in prehistory cannot be exact, but they give the order in which events are thought to have happened.

In 1650, Archbishop James Ussher calculated from the Bible that the Earth was created on Sunday, October 23rd, 4004BC. Today, some people still believe in his date, though most scientists do not.

James Ussher believed he knew when the Earth was created.

Earth's time chart - in seconds

This time chart shows Earth's story since it was formed 4,600 million years ago. It counts each year as if it were only one second.

Formation of the Earth	146 years ago
Earliest known living cells	100 years ago
Jellyfish, corals, sponges	18 years ago
Early reptiles	10 years ago
Dinosaurs, early mammals	6 years ago
First apes	1 year ago
Modern human beings	11 hours ago
Beginning of civilization	2¾ hours ago
Egyptian pyramids built	1¼ hours ago
Birth of Jesus Christ	33 minutes ago
Columbus landed in America	8½ minutes ago
Men landed on the Moon	33 seconds ago

How Do We Know?

Any information we have about prehistory comes from fossils. Fossils are the remains of animals and plants that have become embedded in a hard substance such as rock. Every fossil is a clue to what life was like millions of years ago.

This ammonite fossil is over 65 million years old.

A small chance

The chance of a fossil being found is very small:

• The rock in which it lies must be raised to the surface.

• Wind and rain must then wear the rock away to expose the fossil.

• The fossil must be discovered soon after that before it is worn away.

A fossil is as old as the rock in which it is found. This means that any fossils found in the very bottom layer of rock in the Grand Canyon, USA, will be 2,000 million years old.

Types of fossil

There are three types of fossil:

Body fossils are the actual parts of a prehistoric plant or animal, including any casts or moulds that are made of the dead body. Most body fossils found are of the hard parts of animals such as:

Teeth

Shells

Bones

Fossils of soft body parts are rarely found because these tissues decay easily.

Trace fossils are the imprints or marks made by prehistoric plants and animals while they were still alive, rather than after death. They include:

Skin

Footprints

Droppings

Molecular fossils are chemical traces of prehistoric plants and animals. Scientists crush the rocks which contain the traces so that they can dissolve out and analyse the chemicals.

Becoming a fossil

There are many ways in which a plant or animal can turn into a fossil:

• A small animal or plant becomes trapped in a substance that turns hard.

This prehistoric insect is trapped in amber.

• Minerals seep into rocks, replacing the soft tissues of a buried plant or animal. The mineral forms a rock-like fossil.

• The hard parts of a plant or animal dissolve, leaving only a substance called carbon.

• The hard parts of a plant or animal are replaced by minerals.

• A buried plant or animal dissolves, leaving an impression which may be filled in to make a cast.

This is a fossilized impression of a prehistoric birch leaf.

Living fossils

Many types of animal and plant, such as ferns, dragonflies and some sharks, have changed very little for millions of years. They are called living fossils.*

Great White Shark

Megalodon

Today's Great White Sharks look like much smaller versions of their prehistoric ancestors, called Megalodons.

La Brea Tar Pits, USA, is home to over three million fossils, the oldest of which date back 40,000 years. Tar pits form when oil seeps to the Earth's surface and evaporates, leaving sticky pools. Animals such as lions, wolves and mammoths became trapped in the La Brea pit and their remains were preserved.

Mammoth in a sticky situation

INTERNET LINK
For a link to a Web site where you can watch prehistoric animals turn into fossils in a variety of ways go to
www.usborne-quicklinks.com

Dating fossils

Scientists can work out the age of any fossil up to 100,000 years old by using a process called carbon dating. All living things absorb and then give out rays of carbon particles. After death, the rays are given out at a steady rate. By counting the rays, it is possible to tell how old the fossil is.

Living person	2,500 particle rays per hour
5,600 year old fossil	1,250 particle rays per hour
11,200 year old fossil	625 particle rays per hour
44,000 year old fossil	3 particle rays per hour

* See page 58

Time Trail

Each period of Earth's story has a name. This chart shows the major events that occurred during each period. In this chart (and throughout this book), mya stands for "million years ago".

The Earth began as a cloud of dust and gases swirling round the Sun.

Jurassic
208-145 mya

Dinosaurs increase

Early mammals, 200 mya

Cretaceous
145-65 mya

First bird, 145 mya

Triassic
230-208 mya

First dinosaurs, 215 mya

PANGAEA

The Earth's continents joined up to form one large land mass called Pangaea, 250 mya

Permian
280-230 mya

Early reptiles, 280 mya

Carboniferous
345-280 mya

Tropical forests, 330 mya

First flying insects, 300 mya

INTERNET LINK
For a link to a Web site where you can explore an interactive prehistoric timeline go to **www.usborne-quicklinks.com**

-Cambrian
00-570 mya

Formation of the Earth, 4,600 mya

First known living things, 3,200 mya

First ice age, 2,300 mya

First animals, 680 mya

First shellfish, 570 mya

Cambrian 570-500 mya

Fossils from 208-145 mya were first found in the European Jura mountains, which is why that period is now known as the Jurassic. Many periods on this timescale are named after the places where fossils from that time were first discovered.

Palaeocene 65-55 mya

Earliest primates, 60 mya

Eocene 55-38 mya

Mammals increase.

Oligocene 38-22 mya

Earliest apes, 30 mya

Miocene 22-6 mya

Grazing animals increase.

First arthropods, 570 mya

First fish, 540 mya

Ordovician 500-435 mya

First plants live on land, 420 mya

Pliocene, 6-2 mya

First human beings, 2 mya

Pleistocene, 2 mya-10,000 years ago

Last ice age begins, 100,000 years ago

Holocene, 10,000 ago-the present

First civilizations, 10,000 years ago

Devonian 395-345 mya

First amphibians, 350 mya

Silurian 435-395 mya

First animals live on land, 395 mya

At a glance

To see at a glance the periods covered on each page, look out for timelines like the one below throughout the book.

| Pre-Cambrian | Cambrian |

The Beginning of Life

The first known life on Earth is 3,200 million years old. Fossils of tiny, simple cells were found in cherts (a type of flint) in South Africa. These cells were so small that thousands would have fitted onto the head of a pin.

Plants lived long before the first animals. They made oxygen, which animals breathe to stay alive. Until there was enough oxygen, there could be no animal life.

The first plants made oxygen under water.

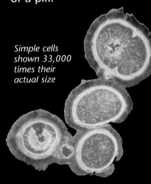
Simple cells shown 33,000 times their actual size

Sunny cells

200 million years after the first known life on Earth, tiny cells, called blue-green bacteria, began to use sunlight and water to make their own food. This process is called photosynthesis and it is how all plants survive. Blue-green bacteria still live today in the same form as they did 3,000 mya.

These blue-green bacteria have been magnified over 1,000 times.

INTERNET LINK
For a link to a Web site where you can take a tour around an exhibit about life on Earth go to **www.usborne-quicklinks.com**

Developing cells

Life developed over millions of years. The first life forms were very simple cells but 2,400 million years later, complex, multi-celled living things began to appear.

Developed	Type of organism	Characteristics
3,200 mya	Prokaryotic cells	Very simple; produce oxygen; offspring are exact copies of themselves
1,500 mya	Eukaryotic cells	Contains specialized structures for different jobs; needs oxygen; offspring are a mixture of both parents
600 mya	Metazoa	Multi-celled organisms

Multi-celled animals

The earliest multi-celled animals can be grouped into three basic categories:

Sponges
These are the simplest multi-celled animals. They pull water through their bodies and filter it for food.

Cnidarians
These include corals, sea anemones and jellyfish. They have sack-like bodies and tentacles to direct food into their mouths.

Worm-like creatures
These animals had fluid-filled cavities inside their bodies. They are now extinct.

Fossils of jellyfish as big as truck wheels were found at Ediacara, Australia. Fossils of soft-bodied animals are rare but the shape of these jellyfish, which were stranded on a beach 670 mya, was preserved by a layer of sand before their bodies rotted.

These soft-bodied animals floated through the Pre-Cambrian waters.

Yet to come...

Here is a list of things that did not yet exist when the Cambrian period ended 550 mya (2,650 million years after the first appearance of life on Earth).

Animals with backbones

Animals with jaws or teeth

Living things on land

Amphibians

Mammals

Reptiles

Insects

Humans

Birds

These sea pens are a type of soft coral.

Shells and Skeletons

The first known shellfish lived in the Cambrian period, 570-500 mya. An enormous number of new animals with shells and skeletons appeared at this time. These creatures made good fossils, so scientists have been able to study their development.

This marella is a relative of the crab.

Shell protection

At the start of the Cambrian period, some worm-like animals began to hunt and eat other animals. They were less likely to eat creatures with shells and skeletons, so more of those creatures survived.

A fossil of a trilobite's protective outer skeleton.

Common fossil

Brachiopods (lampshells) are one of the most commonly found fossils. There are about 300 species of brachiopod living in the seas today but at least 30,000 different species lived in the past.

Brachiopod shells made good fossils.

Our first ancestors?

Chordates are a group of animals which have a stiff rod running down their body. The earliest known chordate is the Chinese cathaymyrus. Humans are also chordates, so this eel-like creature could be one of our first ancestors.

This cathaymyrus dates back 535 million years.

Sponges provided homes and meals for spiny worms.

Some bizarre Cambrian fossils were found in the Burgess Shale rocks in Canada. The fossils show soft-bodied creatures in great detail. In some, the animal's last meal can still be seen inside its body.

This spiky hallucigenia was found in the Burgess Shale.

The Age of Trilobites

The Cambrian period is known as "The Age of Trilobites". Trilobites were among the first arthropods – creatures with jointed legs and outer skeletons. They were usually small, but some grew up to 70cm long, which is around the length of an adult's arm.

Trilobites are related to shrimps and lobsters.

Trilobites were the first animals to have eyes. Human beings have one lens in each eye, but some trilobites had as many as 20,000.

A close-up of a trilobite eye, made up of thousands of lenses

Still here

In the Ordovician and Silurian periods (500-395 mya) yet more creatures with shells and skeletons evolved. They took the place of Cambrian animals that had died out. Some of these replacements are still around today.

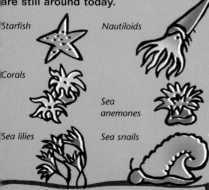

Starfish

Nautiloids

Corals

Sea anemones

Sea lilies

Sea snails

The coral calendar

500 mya, a year lasted for 428 days. How do we know this? Coral grows a fresh band of skeleton every day and the size of each band depends on the season in which it was grown. Scientists are able to calculate how long a prehistoric year lasted by examining the size and number of bands on fossils of coral.

The outer layer of a coral reef

Inside, bands of skeleton grow.

The outer layer of this coral has worn away, leaving only the skeleton.

INTERNET LINK
For a link to a Web site where you can discover why some sea creatures developed shells go to **www.usborne-quicklinks.com**

The First Fish

Fish appeared 540 mya in what is now China. The first fish had no jaws, so ate by sucking in water and filtering out pieces of food.

Jaws

The first fish with jaws appeared during the Silurian period (435-395 mya). They are known as acanthodians, or "spiny sharks", although they were not sharks at all.

Their spiny fins made acanthodians difficult to eat.

Confirmed colour

In 1997, a fossil of a placoderm – a Silurian fish – was found to contain colour cells showing that it had a silver belly and a red back. The placoderm is the oldest ever vertebrate fossil to be found with preserved traces of skin colour.

The placoderm's skin colour may have looked like this.

The first sharks

Sharks first appeared during the Devonian period. A shark's skeleton is made up of cartilage (the same material that is in the tip of your nose).

Cartilage is lighter than bone and this helps sharks to float. Sharks and rays were probably the last major group of fish to evolve.

This early shark's body is streamlined so it can glide through the water.

!

Fish were the first to have a backbone. Animals with a backbone are called vertebrates. Over half of the 42,000 species of vertebrates known in the world are fish.

Ostracoderms — the first animals to have backbones

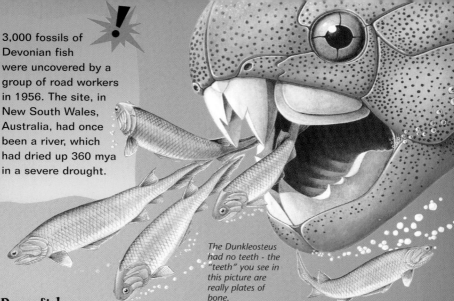

3,000 fossils of Devonian fish were uncovered by a group of road workers in 1956. The site, in New South Wales, Australia, had once been a river, which had dried up 360 mya in a severe drought.

The Dunkleosteus had no teeth - the "teeth" you see in this picture are really plates of bone.

Bony fish

As bony fish developed, they split into two groups:

Ray finned fish have delicate, fan-shaped fins supported by fine, bony rods. Most fish that are alive today are ray fins.

Ray fin

Fleshy finned fish have muscular fins, edged with a fringe of fine rays. These fish developed into the first land-living vertebrates.*

Fleshy fin

Shark-eater

The largest predator of the Devonian seas was the shark-eating Dunkleosteus. It had sharp jaws, but no teeth. Instead of scales, its body was covered with hinged plates.

INTERNET LINK

For a link to a Web site where you can find animations and information about prehistoric sharks go to **www.usborne-quicklinks.com**

Devonian sea monster	Length	Location of fossils	Distinctive features
Dunkleosteus	9m	Africa, Belgium, Morocco, Poland, USA	Heavily armoured; scissor-like jaws
Hyneria lindae	4m	USA	Rough scales; long, sharp teeth
Gyracanthus	2m	Australia, USA, UK	Long spine
Ctenacanthus	nearly 2m	USA, UK	Spines on fins

* See page 21

Plants on Land

For millions of years, the Earth's surface was scorched by the Sun's ultraviolet rays. Nothing could live on land. Simple plants, called algae, grew at the sea's edges, but the rest of the land was rocky and probably bare.

Gradually, a layer of gas called ozone built up around the Earth. It blocked out some of the Sun's rays, enabling plants and animals to live on land.

Plants had been on land for 300 million years before the first flower bloomed. One of the earliest flowering plants was the magnolia. It looked the same as the magnolias we see today.

A modern magnolia flower

Upright plants

To be able to survive on land, plants developed an outer layer to stop them from drying out and inner, woody tubes to carry water through their stems. These tubes keep the plants upright.

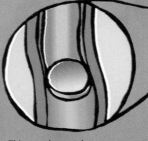

This stem has a tube inside to carry water.

Ferns grew in the hot and steamy prehistoric forests.

The first land plant

The earliest known evidence of plant life on land is a Cooksonia fossil dating back 420 million years. The Cooksonia was simply a stem with a capsule at its tip and had no leaves, roots or flowers.

Cooksonia capsules contained spores.

INTERNET LINK

For a link to a Web site where you can explore pictures and information about the Earth's oldest plants go to **www.usborne-quicklinks.com**

Making coal

Coal is made from prehistoric plants. As plants died, layers of plant material built up, forming peat. The heavy layers above squeezed water and gases out of the peat underneath, and turned it into coal.

Layers of dead plant material covered prehistoric forest floors

The deepest layers formed the coal we mine today.

Familiar plants

The hot, steamy forests and swamps of the Carboniferous period contained some types of plant that can still be found today:

Horsetails

Ferns

Club mosses

Conifers

Spores and seeds

The earliest plants produced tiny cells, called spores. Spores were carried away by the wind or water and then grew into new plants.

During the Devonian period (395-345 mya), some plants, such as seed-ferns, began to produce seeds instead of spores. Seeds are tougher than spores and can grow in drier soil.

This fossil of a seed fern looks very similar to the ferns we see today.

Plant family history

By studying the cells of over 300 modern plants, scientists were able to make a chart to show the order in which modern plants first evolved on land. Green algae in the water evolved into the first land plants – a type of liverwort. All modern land plants are descended from these early liverworts.

A modern liverwort

Timeline of plant evolution

		Flowering plants
		Ferns
		Mosses
		Liverworts
		Green algae
500 mya	250 mya	**Present**

19

Animals on Land

Once plants began to grow on land, there was food for animals to eat. The first creatures to move from water onto land were invertebrates – they did not have backbones.

The first animals to fly were insects. Some were huge. The largest insect ever to have lived was the Meganeura – a giant dragonfly that developed 280 mya.

The Meganeura had a 75cm wingspan – the same as a seagull.

Land crawlers

In the Devonian period (395-345 mya), the most common creatures on land were arthropods – animals with jointed legs and outer skeletons. Many that developed at this time are still common today:

Centipede

Millipede

Spider

Mite

Scorpion

Cockroach

Insect bites

The earliest known insect is a tiny springtail called a Rhyniella. It lived 380 mya among plants found in Rhynie, Scotland. Fossils of these plants had holes showing where the insects had fed.

Rhyniellas – the first known insects

Amber traps

Insect fossils are very rare because their bodies are so delicate. Insects can become fossilized when they are trapped in resin – a sticky liquid which oozes from pine trees. Prehistoric resin turns into a yellow stone, called amber.

A prehistoric insect trapped in amber

Air and water

About 375 mya, an animal called an Icthyostega appeared. It lived mainly in the water but could also breathe air and crawl on land. Animals that live on land but lay their eggs in the water are called amphibians.

Icthyostegas could survive on land...

...and underwater.

The Icthyostega had a strong skeleton to support its large body. Animals that live only in water do not need a strong skeleton because their bodies are supported by the water.

The Icthyostega dragged itself around by its powerful front legs.

The amphibian problem

Early amphibians had the advantage of being able to live both on land and underwater, but there were disadvantages too.

Early amphibians could:	Early amphibians could not:
Breathe air	Mate on dry land
Use their legs and backbones to move around on land	Keep their bodies warm during cold weather
Use their ears to hear sounds in the air	Keep water in their bodies to prevent them from drying out

Growing legs

Scientists believe that amphibians evolved from fleshy finned fish. These fish had lungs and large fins supported by bones and muscles. They could use their fins to push their heads above the water for brief periods. These fins probably developed into amphibian legs.

An amphibian called a Diplocaulus had a boomerang-shaped head that helped it to glide through the water. Its odd shape may have also made the creature difficult for predators to swallow.

The Diplocaulus swam using its head.

INTERNET LINK
For a link to a Web site where you can see how animals arrived on land go to
www.usborne-quicklinks.com

Changing World

The Earth's surface is made up of several huge pieces, called plates. The plates float on a constantly moving layer of rock. Some plates, carried by the rock, are pushed together while others are pulled apart.

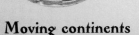

This piece of the Earth's crust is the South American plate.

Land masses on the Earth's surface move along with the plates underneath, drifting at the same speed that your fingernails grow. This movement created the seven continents we know today. They once fitted together like jigsaw pieces, but then drifted apart. This was proved by the discovery of identical plant and animal fossils on the coasts of South America and Africa.

Moving continents

Over millions of years, the movement of the Earth's plates can make the continents drift huge distances.

250 mya, the Earth's three continents collided to make one supercontinent.

By 120 mya, the supercontinent had begun to break up.

By 60 mya, the supercontinent had begun to separate into the seven continents we have today.

Changing climates

The movement of the continents means that the places we know today were very different millions of years ago.

• 450 mya, the Sahara desert was where Antarctica is now and was covered in ice.

• During the Carboniferous period (345-280 mya), Europe and Antarctica were situated on the Equator. This meant that they had very hot climates.

• 200 mya, New York was part of a large lake which was home to the earliest known gliding reptile, called Icarosaurus

• 50 mya, London had a hot and humid climate. It was covered in swamps where crocodiles and turtles lived.

Turtle – an early Londoner

Future shocks

When the Earth's plates scrape against each other, stress builds up in between.

If the pressure becomes too great, energy is released and an earthquake occurs.

Scientists look for damage to rocks to find out where earthquakes struck in prehistoric times. This helps them work out where future earthquakes may happen.

In 1970, scientists discovered that only 6 mya, the Mediterranean Sea was a dry valley. When the Earth's crust moved, the Atlantic Ocean burst over the Straits of Gibraltar in a spectacular waterfall. It took over 100 years to fill the Mediterranean valley with water.

INTERNET LINK

For a link to a Web site where you can see what the Earth looked like in the past and what it may look like in the future go to **www.usborne-quicklinks.com**

Making mountains

When two of the Earth's plates are pushed together, the land crumples up at the edges to form great stretches of mountain. The world's biggest mountain ranges were formed in this way.

Mountain range	When formed	How formed
The Appalachians	300 mya	Africa and North America collided, pushing up the sea floor.
The Ural Mountains	250 mya	Three continents collided to make one large continent, pushing up the land.
The Himalayas	60 mya (and still forming)	India collided with the Asian continent.
The Alps	40 mya (and still forming)	Africa moved north, pushing the Mediterranean sea floor against Europe.
The Andes	15 mya	The Pacific Ocean floor sunk under the edge of South America, pushing up the land.

The Alps began to be made 40 mya and are still forming today.

Before the Dinosaurs

Before dinosaurs appeared, the Earth was inhabited by their earliest relatives. They belonged to a group called amniotes. Amniotes reproduced using eggs containing fluid to protect the growing baby. Today, some amniotes (such as humans) house the growing baby and fluid inside their bodies. Reptiles are one of the earliest amniote groups.

Inside this egg a baby reptile grows, protected from the outside world.

Land lovers

Unlike amphibians, reptiles are able to live on land all the time. This is because they have three major adaptations to life on land that amphibians did not have.

• Scaly skin – reptiles have scaly, waterproof skin to stop their bodies from losing too much water.

• Strong legs – reptiles can lift their bodies off the ground and are able to move around easily on land.

• Eggs with shells – reptile eggs are laid on land and have a waterproof shell that protects the baby.

Sailing back

During the Permian period, a group of amniotes called synapsids developed. Some early synapsids had sails of skin on their backs that they could turn to face the Sun when they needed heat.

This synapsid's sail of skin helped to control its body temperature.

The oldest known fossil eggs in the world were laid by reptiles in the Permian Period (280-230 mya). They were the size of chickens' eggs.

New and improved

About 270 mya, synapsids began to develop longer legs that grew directly underneath their bodies. This allowed them to take bigger strides and move around faster. These new synapsids were called therapsids.

This meat-eating therapsid had long legs for extra speed.

Back to the water

Although reptiles had evolved to cope with life on land, some went back to living in the water. One of the earliest to do this was the Mesosaurus. It returned to the water during the Permian period (280-230 mya).

A Mesosaurus had long, spiky teeth which it used to trap small, shrimp-like creatures in its mouth. It may have had a fin on its tail and webbed feet to help it swim.

The Mesosaurus' feet became webbed to help it swim underwater.

INTERNET LINK

To find a link to a Web site where you can see a therapsid hunting for food, go to **www.usbornequicklinks.com**

Furry friends

By the start of the Triassic period (230 mya), a new type of therapsid, called a cynodont, had emerged. Cynodonts had slim bodies and powerful jaws lined with different types of teeth. Some probably grew fur to keep their bodies warm. By the end of the Triassic period (208 mya), furry cynodonts had developed into a completely new group of amniotes called mammals*.

This cynodont is an ancestor of mammals.

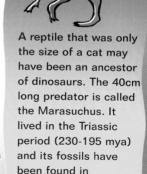

Marasuchus

A reptile that was only the size of a cat may have been an ancestor of dinosaurs. The 40cm long predator is called the Marasuchus. It lived in the Triassic period (230-195 mya) and its fossils have been found in Argentina.

*See page 36

Dinosaur Giants

Dinosaurs are a type of reptile. Most species died out at the end of the Cretaceous period (65 mya), but some dinosaurs are still around today. They can be seen flying through the air, swimming in the water or nesting in trees. This is because all birds are a type of dinosaur.

Great lizards

Dinosaur fossils were first studied by a British scientist called Sir Richard Owen. In 1841, he invented the name dinosaur. The name comes from the Greek *deinos*, which means fearfully great, and *sauros*, which means lizard.

deinos + sauros = fearfully great lizard!

Until around 150 years ago, no one knew that dinosaurs had existed. So when, in 1677, part of a Megalosaurus' leg bone was discovered in England, people thought that it had belonged to a giant human.

Digging up giant bones

Top five dinosaur giants

The longest and heaviest land animals ever to have lived were sauropods. They appeared at the end of the Triassic period (230-208 mya). Sauropods were plant-eaters with large bodies, small heads and extremely long necks and tails.

A 30-tonne Seismosaurus

Sauropod	Weight	Length
Amphicoelias	150 tonnes	60m
Supersaurus	55 tonnes	42m
Argentinosaurus	90 tonnes	41m
Andesaurus	12.5 tonnes	40m
Seismosaurus	30 tonnes	35m

Identity crisis

In 1979, a scientist discovered huge pieces of fossilized dinosaur bone in Colorado, USA. He thought he had discovered a new type of giant dinosaur, measuring 25-30m in length. He named it "Ultrasauros". Later, it was discovered that the bones he found may have belonged to two separate dinosaurs – a Supersaurus and a Brachiosaurus.

The "Ultrasauros" – one dinosaur or two?

Chewing trouble

Sauropods used their long necks to reach the very tops of trees. Their peg-like teeth were good for stripping leaves, but not so good for chewing. This meant they had to swallow tough leaves and twigs without having fully chewed them. They may have swallowed stones to help grind up the food in their stomachs.

High pressure

Some sauropods held their heads high above the ground. To pump blood up the long neck to the brain, they had very large and powerful hearts. Their blood pressure needed to be three or four times as high as a human's.

Diplodocus swallowed tough leaves and twigs.

INTERNET LINK

For a link to a Web site where you can take an interactive journey with a sauropod family go to **www.usborne-quicklinks.com**

Record-breaking body part	Belonged to...	Length (approx)	
Horn	Triceratops	1m	
Claw	Therizinosaurus	70cm	
Neck	Sauroposeidon	15m	
Head	Pentaceratops	3m	
Teeth	Gigantosaurus	15cm	

More Dinosaurs

Over 800 species of dinosaur have been found. Scientists have divided them into two groups, called lizard-hipped and bird-hipped dinosaurs. Lizard-hipped dinosaurs can be identified by their clawed feet and bird-hipped dinosaurs can be identified by their hoofed toes.

Clawed feet

Hoofed toes

Tall tail

The largest meat-eater that has ever lived on land was the fierce Tyrannosaurus rex. It was as long as a humpback whale (around 12.5m) and weighed as much as an African elephant (around 6 tonnes). When walking or running, it had to hold it tail high to balance the weight of its huge head.

Tyrannosaurus rex had a heavy head.

INTERNET LINK
For a link to a Web site where you can explore an amazing dinosaur directory go to
www.usborne-quicklinks.com

Hadrosaurs, also called "duck-bills" because of their broad beaks, had up to 960 teeth in the sides of their jaws at any one time. New teeth grew as others wore out.

Deadliest dinosaurs

The deadliest dinosaurs lived in the Cretaceous period (145-65 mya). Most belonged to a group called dromaeosaurs. They were fast-moving meat-eaters with long claws, sharp teeth and long arms that gave them more stability and mobility when hunting.

These deadly dinosaurs included:

- Dromaeosaurus
- Deinonychus
- Microraptor
- Velociraptor
- Utahraptor

Dromaeosaurs had long arms...

...long claws...

...and very sharp teeth.

Smallest dinosaurs

Fossils of small dinosaurs are very rarely found. This is because small dinosaurs were usually eaten by bigger animals and any remaining traces are difficult to spot. The smallest dinosaurs discovered so far are:

• Saltopus – this insect-eater was 70cm long and about the size of a small cat.

Saltopus

• Compsognathus – this meat-eater was 60cm long and about the size of a chicken.

Compsognathus

• Lesothosaurus – this lizard-like dinosaur was about 1m long and ate plants.

• Microraptor – this bird-like dinosaur was 40cm long and about the size of a crow. It may have spent much of its life in trees.

Microraptor

Lesothosaurus

• Wannanosaurus – this thick-skulled dinosaur was about 60cm long and ate plants.

Wannanosaurus

The Stegosaurus had the smallest brain of any animal compared to its size. Its body was 6m long, but the "thinking" part to its brain was only the size of a walnut.

A walnut

Triceratops' three horns were useful weapons.

What's in a name?

A newly discovered dinosaur is named by the person who finds or classifies it. There are many ways to choose a dinosaur name.

Dinosaur	Reason for name
Triceratops	The three horns on its head
Andesaurus	Fossils first discovered in the Andes mountains in South America
Lambeosaurus	In honour of scientist, Lawrence Lamb
Spinosaurus	The spines on its back
Velociraptor	It could run at high speeds

Dinosaur Lifestyles

Plant-eating dinosaurs needed to defend themselves from predatory meat-eaters. They did this in a number of ways:

• The Polacanthus' weapons were spikes growing on its back and its tail was protected by bony plates.

Spiny back

• The Hypsilophodon was only about 60cm tall. It had long legs and could run quickly to escape from predators.

Long legs

• The Euoplocephalus stunned attackers with a bony club on its tail.

Tail club

• The Stegosaurus was protected by large, bony plates on its back and the spikes on its tail.

Back plates

Head bangers

The Pachycephalosaurus, or bone-headed dinosaur, had a skull up to 25cm thick. It used its skull as a battering ram when it charged, head first, at predators. The males probably also fought each other to attract a mate by proving their strength.

Pachycephalosaurus could use its head as a battering ram.

Running with dinosaurs

Scientists can estimate a dinosaur's speed by examining its body structure and footprints. The bigger dinosaurs could reach high speeds, but only for very short periods.

Dinosaur	Highest speed
Ornithomimus	70kph
Dilophosaurus	65kph
Velociraptor	60kph
Triceratops	30kph
Tyrannosaurus rex	25kph

Some hadrosaurs may have made sounds by blowing air through crests on their heads. The noises could have attracted a mate or warned other hadrosaurs of danger.

Stampede!

Footprints of over 130 stampeding dinosaurs were found in Queensland, Australia. They had been running at a speed of 8kph, chased by a giant meat-eating dinosaur running at 15kph.

INTERNET LINK

For a link to a Web site where you can play a dinosaur survival game go to **www.usborne-quicklinks.com**

Dinosaur nursery

Hundreds of fossilized dinosaur nests, eggs, embryos and babies were found on "Egg Mountain" in Montana, USA. Each nest housed up to 26 eggs. The mountain was once home to 10,000 Maiasaura — a name which means "good mother reptile".

Maiasaura eggs, nests and babies were discovered.

A fossilized "nursery" was found in Montana, USA.

NORTH AMERICA

Montana

Animals in the Sky

Rhamphorhynchus

Around 225 mya, some reptiles developed wings. They are known as pterosaurs. They may have evolved from tree-climbing reptiles which had flaps of skin under their limbs to help them to glide from branch to branch. Pterosaurs are not dinosaurs.

An early gliding reptile

Why fly?

Scientists have many ideas about why some animals began to fly:

• To help move from place to place (by leaping or gliding)

• To free the hind legs for use as weapons

• To help escape from predators

• To reach new food sources or unused living spaces

• To help catch flying or speedy prey

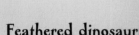

The Pteranodon could swallow a fish whole while in flight.

Central heating

Normally, reptiles rely on the Sun's heat to keep their bodies warm, but pterosaurs could produce their own heat, like birds do. Some pterosaurs were covered with fur, to stop them losing too much heat through their skin.

Pterodactylus

The largest flying animal ever to have lived is a Quetzalcoatlus — a pterosaur the size of a small aircraft. Its fossils were discovered in Texas, USA.

Feathered dinosaur

Most scientists believe that birds are descended from dinosaurs and not from pterosaurs. Modern birds have similar skeletons to some meat-eating dinosaurs.

In the late 1990s, fossils of three new dinosaurs were found in China. The fossils show that they were covered in feathers, but they probably could not fly.

Sinosaupteryx — a feathery dinosaur.

Gliders and fliers

Pterosaurs had light bones and strong muscles which helped them to fly. Those living near water or on cliffs could also glide. They may have glided to save energy so they could stay in the air longer.

Pterodaustro

Flying with pterosaurs

By the Jurassic period, 208 mya, there were several types of pterosaur. They all had big, leathery wings and long necks.

Pterosaur	Developed	Distinguishing features
Rhamphorhynchus	150-145 mya	Pointed jaws to catch fish
Pterodactylus	145 mya	Short tail to help it turn quickly in the air
Pterodaustro	125 mya	Long, curved beak; trapped tiny sea creatures between thin teeth
Pteranodon	85 mya	No teeth, swallowed fish whole
Quetzalcoatlus	70-65 mya	10m wing span

Early bird

The earliest known bird is the Archaeopteryx, which means "ancient wing". It appeared about 145 mya. Although it had feathers and wings like a bird, it also had teeth and a long, bony tail, like a dinosaur.

Although the Archaeopteryx was only the size of a crow, it was probably too heavy to take off from the ground. It may have climbed up trees and launched itself into the air from a high branch.

INTERNET LINK
For a link to a Web site where you can see through a pterosaur's eyes go to **www.usborne-quicklinks.com**

This early bird was a terrible flier.

Animals in the Sea

While dinosaurs were living on land, other reptiles lived in the seas. Their bodies were adapted to life under water, but they still had to come up for air every now and then.

Early sea reptiles

At the start of the Triassic period, 230 mya, there were many types of reptiles living in the sea, such as nothosaurs, placodonts and icthyosaurs.

The Mixosaurus had a fin like a shark's and a mouth like a dolphin's, but it was actually a sea reptile.

Nothosaurs had long, thin bodies that could glide smoothly through the water. They used their big, sharp teeth to catch fish.

Nothosaurs swam using their paddle-like limbs.

Ichthyosaurs had streamlined, dolphin-shaped bodies and large fins that helped them glide swiftly through the water. Their large eyes helped them to see in the dark. They may have searched for food, such as squid, fish and ammonites, in the dark depths of the oceans.

Placodonts were slow-moving reptiles that looked similar to modern turtles. They were usually 1-2m long. Some had bodies covered with plates of bone.

An armoured placodont

Ichthyosaurs flicked their tails from side to side as they swam.

Instead of laying eggs on dry land like other reptiles, ichthyosaurs gave birth to their babies under water. This meant that ichthyosaurs never had to leave the sea.

Monsters of the deep

Some of the biggest sea reptiles belonged to a group called the plesiosaurs. Like modern turtles, they swam using four flippers and probably laid their eggs on beaches.

The Liopleurodon's mouth was 3m long.

Plesiosaur	Length	Distinguishing features
Liopleurodon	12-15m	Large head and short neck; powerful jaws and teeth
Elasmosaurus	14m	Long neck that was half its length
Woolungasaurus	8-10m	Very long neck
Kronosaurus	9m	Very long head; huge, cone-shaped teeth
Muraenosaurus	6m	Long neck and wide body

Sea crocodiles

During the Jurassic period (208-145 mya), crocodiles swam in the sea. Some had flippers instead of limbs and fish-like tails to help them push themselves through the water.

Sea crocodiles could grow up to 7m long.

The pliosaur – a type of plesiosaur – could pick up the scent of other creatures in the sea by filtering water through its mouth and out of its nostrils.

This plesiosaur had a tiny head compared to its large body.

INTERNET LINKS
For a link to a Web site where you can go on an interactive Jurassic sea adventure go to www.usborne-quicklinks.com

Sea survivors

Around 65 mya, almost all sea reptiles died out. Crocodiles and turtles survived, but today, most crocodiles live in fresh water rather than in the sea. Modern-day ocean reptiles include turtles, sea snakes and marine iguanas.

This modern turtle is an ocean reptile.

Most crocodiles live in fresh water.

The Arrival of Mammals

Around 200 mya, a group of creatures called mammals began to appear. They were descended from the cynodonts* that had evolved at the start of the Triassic period.

What is a mammal?

Mammals come in many shapes and sizes, but they all have four things in common:

The rat-like Megazostrodon was one of the earliest mammals.

• They all have hair or bristles on their skin.

• All females feed their babies with milk.

Tree gliders

Some tree-climbing mammals grew flaps of skin between their legs so they could glide, much like the flying squirrels seen today.

• They can all produce their own heat and so stay warm even when the weather is cold.

• They all have several kinds of teeth which they use for cutting and chewing food.

This gliding mammal is an ancestor of the bat.

First mammal facts

The first mammals were insect-eating animals that looked like mice or shrews. For over 100 million years, until the dinosaurs died out, most mammals stayed very small.

Mammal	Developed (period)	Length	Distinguishing features
Megazostrodon	Late Triassic	10cm	Long tail, body and snout
Jeholodens	Middle Cretaceous	13cm	Grasping hands; large eyes
Deltatheridium	Late Cretaceous	15cm	Pouch; sharp teeth
Zalambdalestes	Late Cretaceous	20cm	Upturned snout; interlocking teeth

The first mammals appeared around the same time as the first dinosaurs. They scurried around quietly, usually only coming out at night when most of the other creatures were asleep.

Egg-layers

The first mammals probably all laid eggs, like their reptile relatives did. However, unlike reptiles, mammals fed their young with milk. Today, mammals that lay eggs are called monotremes. The spiny anteater and duck-billed platypus are both monotremes.

These modern mammals are unusual because they lay eggs.

Spiny anteater

Duck-billed platypus

INTERNET LINK
For a link to a Web site where you can go to an early mammal zoo go to **www.usborne-quicklinks.com**

Baby on board

Around 100 mya, some mammals began to give birth to live young instead of laying eggs. The babies crawled up into a pouch on their mother's stomach and continued to grow there. Today, most mammals with pouches are called marsupials.

A few million years after marsupials appeared, placental mammals evolved. Placental females keep their babies inside their bodies until the babies are large enough to survive on their own. Most mammals alive today are placentals.

In times of drought, some marsupials can delay giving birth until the climate improves. The embryo inside the mother's body stops growing. When the weather improves, the embryo begins to grow again and eventually grows big enough to move to its mother's pouch.

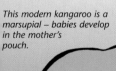
This modern kangaroo is a marsupial – babies develop in the mother's pouch.

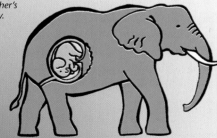
This modern elephant is a placental – babies develop in the mother's body.

* See page 25

More Mammals

After the dinosaurs died out around 65 mya, life became less dangerous for mammals. They began to explore new places to live and to eat a wide range of foods. A huge variety of mammals evolved and spread out all over the world.

An early bat

Meat-eaters

The first meat-eating mammals were called creodonts. They had small brains, short legs and flat feet.

Creodont

Early mammals came in all shapes and sizes.

An early antelope

Gradually, a new group of meat-eaters evolved that were fast-moving, powerful and cunning. These mammals, known as carnivores, had excellent hearing and eyesight and a strong sense of smell.

Modern cats and dogs are descended from an early type of carnivore that only ate insects. They lived around 60-65 mya and looked similar to the civets that are seen today.

An ancient relative of cats and dogs

Plant-eaters

The earliest plant-eating mammals were slow-moving creatures with small brains. They wandered through forests nibbling leaves and plants.

Indricotherium snacking on a tree top

The first deer, cattle, sheep and antelope had all appeared by 25 mya. They roamed over the grasslands in herds. Some of them developed long legs to help them run quickly and horns or antlers which they used to fight off attackers.

INTERNET LINK
For a link to a Web site where you can play a mammal survival game go to **www.usborne-quicklinks.com**

Horse history

The first horses appeared around 50 mya, living in the rainforests of Europe and North America.

• 50 mya, horses were only the size of cats and were sometimes attacked by vicious giant birds.

• By 35 mya, horses had grown longer legs and stronger teeth.

Up until 2 mya, South America was not joined to North America. It had been separate for 60 million years. In that time, many mammals unknown in the rest of the world developed in South America. One such mammal was the giant, armadillo-like Glyptodon.

The Glyptodon was as big as a car.

• By 10 mya, horses had grown to the size of small ponies. They lived in herds on the open plains.

• Around 5 mya, a new kind of horse, called Equus, appeared. Equus is the only kind of horse we see today.

Elephant ancestors

The earliest ancestors of today's elephants were long, pig-like animals that lived in African swamps 40 mya. They spent most of their lives wallowing in water.

An early, pig-like elephant

By 30 mya, elephants had developed short trunks and curved tusks.

By 10 mya, some elephants had spade-like teeth while others had backward-curving tusks.

About 5 mya, a new kind of elephant, called Stegodon, appeared. They looked very similar to today's elephants.

Short tusks and trunk, 30 mya

Backward-curved tusks, 20 mya

Spade-like teeth, 10 mya

Long tusks and trunk, 5 mya

Monster Mammals

Many giant mammals lived in the Pleistocene period (2 mya-10,000 years ago). However, the Uintatherium was one of the earliest giant mammals, having already become extinct by the end of the Eocene period, 38 mya.

The Uintatherium was a plant-eater that weighed over 2 tonnes.

The Megatherium – a Pleistocene mammal – was almost as big as a double-decker bus. Its claws were so huge that it could not put its feet flat on the ground and had to walk on the sides of its feet.

Megatherium walked on the sides of its feet.

Caving in

Fossils of some of the largest land mammals of the Pleistocene period were all found in one hole in the ground. The animals had fallen down the hole in Devon, England, 12,000 years ago. Fossils found included the remains of:

Bison

Elephants

Deer

Bears

Lions

Hippopotamuses

Rhinoceroses

Largest in prehistory	Name	Lived (period)
Sea mammal	Basilosaurus (20m long)	Eocene
Land mammal	Paraceratherium (8m tall, 11m long)	Oligocene
Carnivorous mammal	Megistotherium (6m long, weighed 900kg)	Miocene
Marsupial	Diprotodon (3m long, 2m tall)	Pleistocene
Sabre-toothed tiger	Smilodon (7.5m long, weighed 200kg)	Pleistocene
Mammoth	Imperial mammoth (4.5m tall)	Pleistocene

Smilodon

Giant ancestors

Many mammals living today are descended from giant mammals that lived in the Pleistocene period.

Procoptodon

• The Procoptodon was the largest kangaroo ever known. It was three times taller and heavier than the biggest of today's kangaroos.

• The Gigantopithecus was a great ape that was twice as tall and twice as heavy as a modern male gorilla.

Gigantopithecus lived on the forest floor as it was too heavy to climb trees.

• The Glyptodon was an armadillo-like creature the size of a small car.

• The cave bear was a powerful animal that weighed 1 tonne.

Cave bear

• The giant beaver was as long and heavy as a modern polar bear with a tail measuring 0.5m.

INTERNET LINK

For a link to a Web site where you can find pictures, movies and fact files about the monster mammals of the last ice age go to **www.usborne-quicklinks.com**

• The Megaceros was the biggest deer ever known. It was as tall as two men. The male's antlers had the widest span of any known animal. They were 3m wide and weighed 50kg.

• The cave lion was the biggest lion ever known. It could grow up to twice as long as today's African lions.

The biggest prehistoric mammals lived on the largest continents – North America and Asia. They were so huge that they had to live in large, open spaces to avoid overcrowding.

Woolly mammoths flourished in North America during the last ice age.

• The woolly rhino was twice as heavy as a modern black rhino. Its main horn was 1m long.

The woolly rhino used its horn to dig up food.

Ice Ages

Several times in the Earth's past, large parts of the world have been buried under thick sheets of ice. Each time, the ice has stayed frozen for thousands of years. These long, freezing periods are known as ice ages.

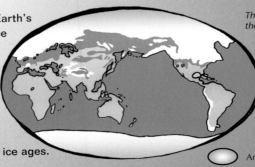

The Earth during the last ice age

○ Area covered in ice

○ Frozen lands where animals could live

The last ice age

The last ice age began 100,000 years ago and ended 10,000 years ago. At its peak, around 21,000 years ago, thick masses of ice covered much of North America, Europe and Asia. Almost one third of the Earth's land surface was covered by ice.

INTERNET LINK
For a link to a Web site where you can travel back in time to the last ice age go to www.usborne-quicklinks.com

Freezing reasons

The exact reasons why ice ages occur are not fully known, but there are likely to be a number of causes, such as:

• the changes in ocean circulation

• the position of the continents

• the amount of heat from the Sun trapped in the Earth's atmosphere

• the concentration of gases in the Earth's atmosphere

Bridging the gap

As sea water turned to ice in the last ice age, the world's sea level lowered at a rate of 12m every 1,000 years. This created land bridges between places that had been separated by sea. Animals could then migrate to other continents. Bridges were created between Britain and the rest of Europe, Alaska and Siberia, and Africa and Europe.

Falling sea levels exposed areas of land that had been under water.

Living on the edge

At the start of the last ice age, many animals moved to warmer areas but some stayed in the frozen lands, called tundra, near the edge of the ice sheets. The animals that lived there became adapted to life in a cold environment.

The woolly rhinoceros had a useful horn.

Animal	Adaptation
Woolly mammoth	Body covered with thick hair to keep it warm
Arctic hare	Body covered with white fur to help it hide in the snow
Woolly rhinoceros	Used its horn to brush aside snow to reach underlying vegetation
Cave bear	Sheltered in caves during the harsh winters

Ice traps

Sometimes animals fell into swamps which later froze solid. The animals' bodies were trapped in ice and could not rot away, remaining preserved for thousands of years. In the last 300 years, 4,700 frozen mammoths have been found in the icy ground of Siberia, in northern Russia.

 A frozen mammoth found in 1900 in Siberia, still had 14kg of undigested food in its stomach. The mammoth was so well preserved 30,000 years after being frozen, that people were able to eat some of its meat.

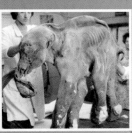

This frozen baby mammoth was found in Siberia in 1977.

Disappearing act

At the end of the last ice age, around 10,000 years ago, many animals died out. No one knows exactly why this happened, but one reason might have been the change in the weather, which caused the ice sheets to melt. Some animals, such as mammoths, were hunted by early humans, and this could be another reason why they disappeared.

Early human hunters may have caused the extinction of the mammoths.

Extinction

At different times in the Earth's past, groups of animals and plants have died out suddenly. Listed below are examples of species that died out during major extinctions at the end of six prehistoric periods:

Cambrian (ended 500 mya) — Many trilobites

Ordovician (ended 435 mya) — Many nautiloids

Devonian (ended 345 mya) — Many placoderms

Permian (ended 230 mya) — Most reptiles

Triassic (ended 208 mya) — Many sponges

Cretaceous (ended 65 mya)

All dinosaurs except birds

Biggest extinction

At the end of the Permian period, 230 mya, many plants and animals suddenly died out.
It was the biggest mass extinction the world has ever known and caused the death of:

- 29% of insect species

- 67% of amphibian species

- 78% of reptile species

- Most of the land plants

All these species died out over a period of just one million years.

The Cretaceous extinction wiped out most of the dinosaurs.

About 99% of all plant and animal species that have ever lived are now extinct. There are about five million species living today, but if no species had ever become extinct, there would be 980 million.

Minor extinctions

Since the last major extinction, about 65 mya, there have been many minor extinctions. Over the last 2.5 million years, various creatures have become extinct, from large mammals to small molluscs. The most serious mammal extinction happened 10,000 years ago, at the end of the last ice age.*

Mammoths died out at the end of the last ice age.

 * See page 42

Explaining extinction

Scientists have four main explanations for why mass extinctions occur:

The Asteroid Theory – a huge asteroid hits the Earth, producing a dust cloud that blocks out all sunlight. It may also cause earthquakes and tidal waves.

The Climate Change Theory – many creatures die out because they cannot adjust to long periods of heavy rainfall or to the beginnings and ends of ice ages.

The Volcano Theory – rock pours out from the Earth's crust, throwing up dust and smoke that blocks out all sunlight and acid that poisons the oceans.

The Sea Level Change Theory – many creatures die out because they cannot adjust to the disruption of their habitats caused by changes in sea level.

Most animals that weighed over 10kg died at the end of the Cretaceous period. But all small insects and some small birds, lizards and sea creatures survived. Why most of the larger animals died out and the smaller ones didn't, is a mystery.

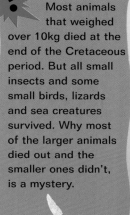

The dragonfly is a survivor.

Dinosaur death

Many other reasons have been suggested for why the dinosaurs died out, including:

- diseases
- over-eating
- infertility
- poisonous plants
- their eggs eaten by birds or mammals.

INTERNET LINK
For a link to a Web site where you can find information about extinction go to **www.usborne-quicklinks.com**

Period of extinction	Probable causes
Cambrian	Climate change, Sea level change
Ordovician	Climate change, Sea level change
Devonian	Climate change
Permian	Asteroid, Volcano, Climate change, Sea level change
Triassic	Climate change
Cretaceous	Asteroid, Volcano

Our Ancestors

Over millions of years, a group of mammals called primates developed into the first human beings. The earliest primates were small, squirrel-like creatures that scurried around in trees.

This Plesiadapis is one of your early relatives.

Shrinking snouts

Most early primates had long noses, or snouts, for sniffing out food. Some later primates relied on their eyes instead of their noses to find food, so their snouts gradually became shorter.

From long snout to stubby nose

Apes and monkeys

The first monkeys and apes evolved from primates around 30 mya. The earliest monkeys were expert tree-climbers and some developed long tails for grasping branches. Apes were bigger and stronger than monkeys. They had broad chests and strong arms which helped them to swing from tree to tree.

Two early apes grooming

Almost human

By 14 mya, some primates had developed many human-like features:

• Their eyesight developed so that they could see shapes and judge distances better.

• They began to walk on two feet instead of walking on all fours.

• Their paws had developed into fingers and toes with sensitive tips.

• They lived in groups and looked after each other, spending a long time showing their children how to survive.

The first humans to discover fire probably could not light fires for themselves. They may have found fires that had started when lightning struck dry grass and then carried a burning branch away to a cave or camp. They could have kept the same fire burning for days, or even weeks.

INTERNET LINK

For a link to a Web site where you can journey through human evolution go to **www.usborne-quicklinks.com**

Walking upright

Primates that walk upright (including humans) are called hominids. The most famous set of hominid bones is an Australopithecus skeleton from Ethiopia. The skeleton has been named "Lucy".*

A group of Australopithecus – the earliest hominids – using sticks to hunt termites.

Name of primate	Lived	Average size	Major achievement
Sivapithecus	14-8 mya	90 cm tall, weighed 12kg	This early ape could walk short distances on two feet and used its hands to carry food.
Australopithecus	5-1.5 mya	1.2m tall weighed 23kg	This man-ape was the first primate to walk upright.
Homo habilis	2-1.5 mya	1.5m tall weighed 45kg	This earliest human began making stone tools to strip meat from animal carcasses.
Homo erectus	1.5 mya-200,000 years ago	1.6m tall weighed 60kg	This upright man hunted large animals and used fire for cooking and keeping warm.
Homo sapiens neanderthalensis	200,000-40,000 years ago	1.7m tall weighed 70kg	This Neanderthal man made clothes and shelters from animal skins.
Homo sapiens sapiens	40,000 years ago-the present	1.8m tall weighs 70kg	This modern man developed a spoken language to communicate with others.

Sivapithecus used its hands to carry food.

Homo habilis made stone tools.

Homo erectus used fur to make clothes.

Pliocene   Pleistocene   * See page 48

Famous Finds

Scientists have been finding fossils of early humans all over the world for over a hundred years. Many important fossils have been found around the Great Rift Valley in Africa. Early human fossils were first found there in 1958 and discoveries are still being made there today.

The red mark on this map of Africa shows where the Great Rift Valley lies.

So far, Africa is the only continent where our earliest human ancestors (Australopithecus and Homo habilis) have been discovered.

The skull of one of our African ancestors

Amazing trace fossils were found here in South Africa. Follow the footprints to find out more...

INTERNET LINK
For a link to a Web site where you can follow a timeline of human fossil discovery go to **www.usborne-quicklinks.com**

Fossil footprints

In 1997, scientists discovered a trail of fossilized footprints on the shore of a South African lagoon. They are thought to have been left by a Homo sapiens sapiens 117,000 years ago. The footprints are the earliest known trace fossils of modern human beings.

The biggest hoax in the history of fossil finds took place in 1912, when a supposedly human fossil was found in a gravel pit in Piltdown, England. The fossil came to be known as "Piltdown Man". After 40 years of fame, it was found to be a fake. The skull's jaw was from a 500 year old orang-utan.

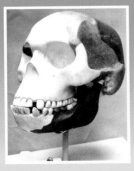

The Piltdown Man's skull was not entirely human.

48

Oldest inhabitants

• The oldest Australian human fossils are bones belonging to a 60,000 year old Neanderthal found in Southeastern Australia. It was nicknamed "Mungo Man".

Mungo Man may have looked like this.

• The oldest Asian human fossil is the skull of a 2 million year-old Homo erectus. It was nicknamed "Java Man".

• The oldest European human fossils are two skulls that probably date back over 1.5 million years, found in the former Republic of Georgia.

• The oldest American human fossil is an 11,500 year-old skull found in Brazil. It was nicknamed "Luiza".

• The oldest British human fossils are a limb bone and tooth that belonged to a 500,000 year-old Homo erectus that was nicknamed "Boxgrove Man".

Fossils found	When	Where
The first Homo erectus bones to be discovered	1891	Java
Neanderthal skeleton	1908	France
14 skullcaps, several facial, jaw and limb bones, and the teeth of 40 Homo erectus individuals	1927	China
A 2 million year old Homo erectus child's skull	1936	Java
Nine skeletons in a Neanderthal burial site	1957	Iraq
A 3 million year old Australopithecus skeleton that came to be known as "Lucy"	1974	Ethiopia
An Australopithecus skeleton – the most complete skeleton ever found.	1998	South Africa
A 3.5 million year old skull of a new type of man-ape, given the name Kenyanthropus platyops	2001	Kenya
A 7 million year old skull of a possible hominid, given the name Sahelanthropus tchadensis	2002	Chad

This Neanderthal was buried with flowers, tools and bones.

His remains were found in a Neanderthal burial site in Iraq.

Dragon bones

Local people around Choukoutien in China found pieces of bone in caves near their village. They called them "dragon bones" and used them in herbal remedies. In 1927, some of the bones were found to belong to a new species of Homo erectus that lived in the area 500,000-250,000 years ago. It came to be known as "Peking Man".

Peking Man was mistaken for a dragon.

Finding Food

The first modern people hunted animals and gathered plants to eat. They moved from place to place in search of food. People who live like this are called hunter-gatherers.

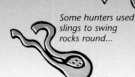

Some hunters used slings to swing rocks round...

...and then let them go, hoping to hit a bird.

Scientists once thought that our ancestors were cannibals. They found fossils of Homo erectus skulls that were broken as if to take out the brains, and bones, smashed for the marrow inside. It was thought that humans had eaten the brains and marrow as part of a ritual, but it is now believed that the injuries were caused by cave bears.

Broken skulls caused confusion about cannibals.

Herd followers

Hunter-gatherers had to follow the herds of wild animals they hunted. Some European and Asian tribes followed herds of animals, such as reindeer and bison, all year round. The animals led them to new places.

Hunters followed herds of bison.

INTERNET LINK

For a link to a Web site where you can become a hunter-gatherer go to **www.usborne-quicklinks.com**

The spear is attached to a spur sticking out of the spear-thrower.

Mammoth hunters

During the last ice age, tribes living on the frozen plains of Eastern Europe became experts at hunting mammoths. They used a weapon called a spear-thrower, which allowed them to attack mammoths from a safe distance.

The hunter grips onto the spear-thrower and hurls the spear forward.

Early farmers discovered how to sow seeds...

...and reaped the rewards when harvest time came.

Settling down

Around 10,000 years ago, the last ice age came to an end. Forests began to grow where ice had been. Tribes of people found places where they could hunt, catch fish and grow plants all year round.

Domestic changes

Plants and animals grown and bred by people are described as domesticated. Over time, domesticated species change from their wild ancestors.

The horse in this Pleistocene carving must be domesticated because it is wearing a harness.

Plant	First domesticated	Place
Wheat	10,000 years ago	Iraq
Barley	10,000 years ago	Turkey
Rice	8,000 years ago	Thailand
Corn	7,500 years ago	Mexico
Potatoes	4,000 years ago	Argentina

Animal	First domesticated	Place
Sheep	10,000 years ago	Iraq
Pig	9,000 years ago	Iran
Cattle	8,000 years ago	Turkey
Camel	5,000 years ago	Saudi Arabia
Horse	5,000 years ago	Russia

Hunter-gatherer's menu

Fresh oysters
Raw seagull eggs

Elephant steak
Roast rhino rump
Roast camel hump

served with leaves, roots, berries, fruit

Mammoth Hunter's Menu

Mixed salad of shellfish

Woolly mammoth steak
Roast reindeer leg
wild boar chop
eggs, roots and tubers

Fruit and maple sap

Early Farmer's Menu

Bread and Olives

Sliced Goose breast
Roast leg of mutton
Stewed beef, peas,
lentils and onions

Dates Apples
Grapes

Making Things

Human prehistory is divided into Ages, according to the tools early people made at the time. Tools developed at different times in different places. For example, the Neolithic Age began 10,000 years ago in the Middle East, but only reached Britain 6,000 years ago.

Stone hand-axe

Wooden ladle

Harpoons made from bone and wood

Clay pot

Periods of the Stone Age

The Stone Age is the earliest period in human prehistory, when people made tools and weapons only out of stone and bone. It is divided into five periods:

Period	Began (years ago)	Type of human	Tools invented
Lower Palaeolithic	600,000	Homo erectus	Hand-axes
Middle Palaeolithic	220,000	Neanderthal	Flake tools (for cutting)
Upper Palaeolithic	35,000	Homo sapiens	Harpoons, knives
Mesolithic	12,000	Homo sapiens	Fish hooks, arrow heads, combs, needles, boats
Neolithic	10,000	Homo sapiens	Daggers, ladles, pots

Skis made during the Upper Palaeolithic were found in Russia. They were made from bone and decorated with an elk-head design.

Made from mammoths

During the last ice age, tribes of mammoth-hunters made almost everything they needed from mammoths' bodies. They made tents, clothes, weapons and even musical instruments out of mammoth bones and skins.

Hunters used mammoth bones and animal fur to make huts.

The earliest...

...cloth
Pieces of the oldest known cloth were found in Israel. They are 9,000 years old and have 11 different patterns.

...musical instruments
Flutes and whistles were used 20,000 years ago, either to make music or as signals during hunts. Flutes were made of bird and bear bones, and whistles from the toe bones of deer.

...clothes
A 37,000 year-old body was found in the frozen soil of Siberia, wearing a shirt and trousers made from animal skins.

...sails
Sailing boats were first used in the Middle East 5,000 years ago.

Early clothes were made from skins and stitched with thongs.

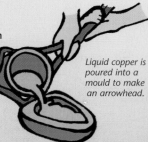
The first flutes and whistles were made from animal bones.

INTERNET LINK
For a link to a Web site where you can find out about Stone Age hand-axes go to **www.usborne-quicklinks.com**

The Metal Ages

For 98% of the time human beings have been on Earth, they have lived in the Stone Ages, using stone, wood and bone tools. They first learned to make tools from metal about 9,000 years ago.

Liquid copper is poured into a mould to make an arrowhead.

The oldest known wheel is about 5,500 years old. It was found in the Middle East. The first wheels were made in three stages:

1. A log was cut into rectangular sections.

2. Three rounded pieces were carved out of each section.

3. The three pieces were fixed together to make a wheel.

Age:	Began Middle East:	Began Europe:
Copper	9,000 years ago	5,000 years ago
Bronze	6,000 years ago	5,000 years ago
Iron	2,900 years ago	2,600 years ago

Building Things

In Europe, prehistoric people built huge mounds of earth and stones, called barrows, over graves. The largest one is Silbury Hill in England. It is 40m high and it covers an area of 20,000m squared. About 670,000 tonnes of chalky earth were moved to make the barrow. It would have taken the equivalent of 3,700 men 600 days to build.

This person is buried under a barrow.

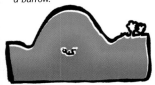

Standing stones

About 4,500 years ago, prehistoric people set up large standing stones, called menhirs. Today, 3,000 menhirs still stand in Carnac, France. They form parallel lines which stretch for 6km. No one knows why the stones were put there.

The Celtic word menhir means "long stone".

One of the biggest menhirs (now broken) was about 20m high – over three times as tall as a giraffe – and weighed roughly 350 tonnes. It can be found at Locmariaquer, France.

Mystery monument

Over 4,000 years ago, a stone monument was built on Salisbury Plain, England. Who built it and why remains a mystery. The monument is called Stonehenge.

Stonehenge took 1,700 years to build. The upright stones, each weighing over 50 tonnes, were moved from 40km away. The stones for the cross pieces came from Wales, 220km away. It would have taken at least 1,000 men to drag each stone.

Nobody knows who built Stonehenge or why.

Stones were dragged along on rollers

Stonehenge would have looked like this when it was first built.

Branch and skin tents were temporary shelters.

First shelters

The first shelters were made by hunter-gatherers 40,000 years ago. They were tent-like constructions made from branches and animal skins. The shelters were only temporary because hunter-gatherers moved from place to place to find food.

INTERNET LINK

For a link to a Web site where you can take a tour round an ancient Turkish village go to **www.usborne-quicklinks.com**

Farming villages

Once people knew how to farm they no longer needed to move around to hunt for food. They began to settle down in villages, making houses from clay bricks. Early villages were enclosed by high clay walls for protection against wild animals.

A busy farming village

Woven walls

The early Greeks built houses out of wattle and daub – sticks woven together and plastered over with mud. The roofs were thatched with grass and there was a hole in the top through which smoke could escape.

A stick framework, covered with mud

Village	Country	Built (approx. years ago)
Jericho	Jordan	10,000
Çatal Hüyük	Turkey	8,500
Dimini	Greece	7,000
Pan P'o Ts'un	China	7,000
Vinca	Serbia	7,000

Close quarters

The houses of the prehistoric Turkish village of Çatal Hüyük were closely packed together. There were no streets, but people could move from house to house by climbing ladders that hung from the roofs.

Çatal Hüyük

Artists and Writers

Early cave paintings show mostly animals such as bison, deer, horses and mammoths. The painters may have believed that the pictures would help them catch the animals they hunted.

Powder paints

Cave-painters made paints from minerals ground into powder. Red, yellow and brown paint was made from ochre (a mineral found in clay) and black was made from charcoal. The powder was mixed with water or fat, and painted with brushes or pads of animal fur.

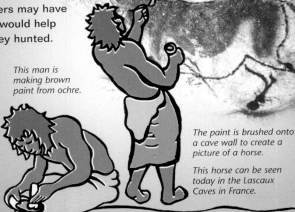

This man is making brown paint from ochre.

The paint is brushed onto a cave wall to create a picture of a horse.

This horse can be seen today in the Lascaux Caves in France.

INTERNET LINK
For a link to a Web site where you can see prehistoric art from around the world go to **www.usborne-quicklinks.com**

When out hunting, prehistoric men often took carved images of very fat and pregnant women with them. The statues, made out of stone or ivory, symbolized health and fertility. They may have carried the statues to bring them good luck in their search for food.

This fat woman may have been a good luck charm.

Strung together

Early people made necklaces by stringing together animal teeth, stones, shells, fishbones and pieces of eggshell. These were probably worn for religious ceremonies and tribe leaders may have had their own special necklaces.

The beads on this necklace are made from shells.

Oldest art	How old?	Where found
Necklaces	35,000 years	Czech Republic
Paintings	30,000 years	On cave walls in France and Spain
Sculptures	30,000 years	Austria
Written song	4,000 years	Syria

Where writing began	When writing began
Iraq	5,500 years ago
Egypt	5,000 years ago
Indus Valley	4,600 years ago
Crete	4,000 years ago
China	3,500 years ago

This bone is engraved with the first known example of Chinese writing.

Symbols from ancient Indus Valley writing

Writing in clay

The first words were written about 5,500 years ago in Iraq. There were no separate letters; each word was a picture of an object. They were scratched onto wet clay tablets which were then dried.

Later, writers used a wedge-shaped stick to mark the clay. This writing is called cuneiform (from the Latin word for "wedge-shaped"). It stood for sounds as well as objects.

Writing from Crete, 4000 years ago

This man is flattening out clay to make tablets.

He draws picture signs onto the wet clay with a stiff reed.

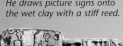

Cuneiform writing on clay tablets.

The picture signs in hieroglyphics (ancient Egyptian writing) can be written from left to right or right to left. The way the pictures of men or animals are facing show which way the message should be read.

This is read from left to right.

This is read from right to left.

For the record

30,000 year-old bones provide the oldest evidence of record-keeping. The bones, found in Cromagnon, France, were engraved with a series of lines. Prehistoric people may have engraved them to record the cycle of the moon, or perhaps the number of animals killed in a hunt.

Prehistoric Survivors

Some plants and animals have remained relatively unchanged for millions of years. Studying these living fossils can help scientists understand what prehistoric plants and animals looked like and how they lived.

Nautilus

Permanent plants

Gingko – this tree has survived almost unchanged for the last 195 million years.

Gingko leaves may have been eaten by dinosaurs.

Metasequoia – this pine tree (also called Dawn Redwood) first grew on Earth 100 mya.

Cycad – this spiky plant has a fossil record 280 million years old.

Magnolia – the first magnolia trees grew 120 mya. They produced some of the first flowers.

Magnolia – an early flower

Monkey puzzle – this tree has a fossil record that dates back 250 million years.

Keep crawling

Cockroach – the first cockroach appeared on Earth 345 mya.

Cockroaches – prehistoric pests

Silverfish – this insect has remained unchanged for 395 million years.

Silverfish

Velvet worm – this caterpillar-like animal lives in the rainforest. Its ancestors crawled on the sea-floor 500 mya.

Still swimming

Nautilus – found in the Indian Ocean, this sea animal first appeared on Earth 50 mya.

Horseshoe crab – found along the Atlantic coast of the USA, this sea creature first lived on Earth 300 mya.

Australian lungfish – this fish has been on Earth for 225 million years.

Crocodile – this reptile's fossil record dates back 200 million years.

Turtle – the first turtle appeared 275 mya.

Lingula – this lampshell has one of the longest fossil records of any animal, dating back 570 million years.

Lingulas were among the first sea creatures.

INTERNET LINK
For a link to a Web site where you can find pictures and profiles of living fossils go to **www.usborne-quicklinks.com**

Back to life

Some plants and animals alive today were once believed to have been extinct for millions of years, only to be found alive in remote parts of the world.

In 1994, an unusual pine tree was found growing in an Australian National Park. The tree, which came to be known as the Wollemi Pine, was thought to have died out 65 mya. It is now one of the world's rarest species with only 43 adult trees known.

A modern Wollemi Pine leaf with its fossil ancestors.

Okapis were thought to be extinct mammals that had evolved into horses 30 mya. Then, in 1900, okapis were discovered alive and well in Africa.

Okapis are very shy and are hard to spot in the wild.

Coelacanth

Odd-looking, blue fish were sometimes caught off the coast of Madagascar. Locals used their skin as sandpaper. In 1938 one of the fish was identified by scientists to be a coelacanth – a creature thought to have been extinct for 70 million years.

Some people believe that there is a prehistoric monster still living in Loch Ness, Scotland. There have even been sightings of a long-necked creature in the loch. Some think that it might be a type of plesiosaur that first appeared on Earth 60 mya.

Survival tips

Most species of living fossil have survived with little change through periods of severe climate change and mass extinction. Some animals have achieved this by being able to:

• live anywhere – horseshoe crabs and cockroaches can survive extreme temperatures.

Horseshoe crab

• go without food – horseshoe crabs can go for a full year without eating.

• eat anything – cockroaches and crocodiles can eat a wide variety of food.

• heal quickly – crocodiles are tough creatures that can survive serious injuries.

Crocodiles are as tough as they look.

Glossary

Amniotes A group of animals that reproduce using eggs that contain fluid to protect the growing embryo.

Amphibians A group of animals that live both on land and in water.

Ancestor An animal or plant that is directly related to another at a later point in time.

Arthropods A group of animals with jointed legs and outer skeletons.

Asteroid A rocky object, smaller than a planet, which circles the Sun.

Atmosphere The mixture of gases that surrounds a planet, such as the air around Earth.

Bacteria Very small living things that live in the air, water and ground and in plants and animals.

Barrow A mound of earth and stones built over graves in prehistoric times.

Cell The smallest basic unit of a plant or animal.

Climate The usual weather conditions of a particular place.

Continent A large land mass on the Earth's surface mainly surrounded by ocean.

Descendant An animal or plant which has developed from its ancestor.

Dinosaur A type of reptile with upright hind legs, a strong pelvis and a flexible neck.

Embryo An animal growing in its mother's womb or in an egg.

Equator An imaginary line drawn around the middle of the Earth an equal distance from the North Pole and the South Pole.

Evaporate To change from a liquid to a gas.

Evolve To develop gradually.

Extinction When a group of plants or animals dies out.

Fossil The remains of an animal or plant that has become embedded in rock.

Habitat The natural surroundings in which an animal or plant lives.

Herd Animals that live and feed as a group.

Hominid A type of mammal that is able to walk upright, including apes and humans.

Living fossil A species of plant or animal that has remained relatively unchanged since prehistoric times.

Mammals A group of warm-blooded vertebrates that have hair and feed their young on milk from their bodies.

Menhir A large standing stone erected by people in prehistoric times.

Migrate To travel to a different place in order to live there.

Mineral A naturally occurring chemical found in crystal form in the ground.

Mya Million years ago

Predator An animal that hunts, kills and eats other animals.

Prehistory The story of life on Earth from the first living things to the earliest known writing.

Prey An animal that is hunted for food by other animals.

Reptiles A group of animals with scaly, waterproof skin, including snakes and dinosaurs.

Species A group of animals or plants which have similar features and are able to mate with each other.

Tribe A group of people who live together, sharing the same language, culture and history.

Ultraviolet A type of light that is beyond violet in the spectrum.

Vertebrates A group of animals with backbones.

Volcano A mountain with a large hole at the top which can force out hot rock, gases and dust.

Using the Internet

Internet links

Most of the Web sites described in this book can be accessed with a standard home computer and an Internet browser (the software that enables you to display information from the Internet). We recommend:

• A PC with Microsoft® Windows 98 or later version, or a Macintosh computer with System 9.0 or later, and 64Mb RAM
• A browser such as Microsoft® Internet Explorer 5, or Netscape® 6, or later versions
• Connection to the Internet via a modem (preferably 56Kbps) or a faster digital or cable line
• An account with an Internet Service Provider (ISP)
• A sound card to hear sound files

Extras

Some Web sites need additional free programs, called plug-ins, to play sounds, or to show videos, animations or 3-D images. If you go to a site and you do not have the necessary plug-in, a message saying so will come up on the screen. There is usually a button on the site that you can click on to download the plug-in. Alternatively, go to **www.usborne-quicklinks.com** and click on "Net Help". There you can find links to download plug-ins. Here is a list of plug-ins you might need:

RealPlayer® – lets you play videos and hear sound files
QuickTime – lets you view video clips
Shockwave® – lets you play animations and interactive programs
Flash™ – lets you play animations

Help

For general help and advice on using the Internet, go to **Usborne Quicklinks** at **www.usborne-quicklinks.com** and click on **Net Help**. To find out more about how to use your Web browser, click on **Help** at the top of the browser, and then choose Contents and Index. You'll find a huge searchable dictionary containing tips on how to find your way around the Internet.

Internet safety

Remember to follow the Internet safety guidelines at the front of this book. For more safety information, go to **Usborne Quicklinks** and click on **Net Help**.

Computer viruses

A computer virus is a program that can seriously damage your computer. A virus can get into your computer when you download programs from the Internet, or in an attachment (an extra file) that arrives with an e-mail. We strongly recommend that you buy anti-virus software to protect your computer, and that you update the software regularly.

INTERNET LINK
To find a link to a Web site where you can find out more about computer viruses, go to **www.usborne-quicklinks.com** and click on **Net Help**.

Macintosh and QuickTime are trademarks of Apple Computer, Inc., registered in the U.S. and other countries.
RealPlayer is a trademark of RealNetworks, Inc., registered in the U.S. and other countries.
Flash and Shockwave are trademarks of Macromedia, Inc., registered in the U.S. and other countries.

Index

Acknowledgements

Every effort has been made to trace the copyright holders of the material in this book. If any rights have been omitted, the publishers offer to rectify this in any subsequent editions following notification. The publishers are grateful to the following organizations and individuals for their permission to reproduce material (t=top, m=middle, b=bottom, l=left, r=right):

Corbis: **7bl** Bettmann/CORBIS; **15ml** Layne Kennedy/CORBIS; **23b** Nathan Benn/CORBIS; **43ml** Bettmann/CORBIS; **48br** Bettmann/CORBIS; **54m** Adam Woolfitt/CORBIS; **54bl** John Noble/CORBIS; **56tr** Bettmann/CORBIS
Digital Vision: **1 background**; **2-3 background**; **6bl**; **6-7 background**; **7 br**; **18-19 background**; **35m**; **59br**
Science Photo Library: **12l** Dr Kari Lounatmaa/Science Photo Library; **12r** Sinclair Stammers/Science Photo Library; **15tr** Sinclair Stammers/Science Photo Library; **15br** Victor Habbick Visions/Science Photo Library
Wildlight Photo Agency: **59ml**

Additional illustrators John Barber, Gary Bines, Giacinto Gaudenzi, Tony Gibson, Laura Hammonds, Bob Hersey, Phillip Hood, Inklink Firenze, Ian Jackson, Kevin Maddison, Peter Massey, Sean Milne, Luis Rey, Andrew Robinson, Luke Sargent, Chris Shields, Rod Sutterby, Franco Tempesta, David Wright

Additional designers Adam Constantine, Laura Hammonds and Joanne Kirkby

Material in this book is based on *The Usborne Book of Prehistoric Facts and Lists* by Annabel Craig, © Usborne Publishing, 1986.